Kate Shelley and the
Midnight Express

by Margaret K. Wetterer
illustrations by Karen Ritz

Orlando   Boston   Dallas   Chicago   San Diego

Visit *The Learning Site!*

www.harcourtschool.com

For Margaret Kelly Eason and her grandfather — M.K.W.

For my Iowa friends, the Lynches and the Odlands — K.R.

Many people and organizations generously helped in gathering material on the Kate Shelley story. The author would like to express her thanks to all of them, and especially to the staff of the Huntington (New York) Public Library; the Boone County Historical Society, Boone, Iowa; the Association of American Railroads; Kappa Kappa Gamma Fraternity, which Kate joined while attending Simpson College, Iowa; the United Transportation Union of the Chicago and Northwestern Transportation Company; the Iowa State Department of History and Archives; and Kate Shelley's nephew, Mr. John D. (Jack) Shelley of Ames, Iowa.

This edition is published by special arrangement with Carolrhoda Books, Inc.

Grateful acknowledgment is made to Carolrhoda Books, Inc.
for permission to reprint *Kate Shelley and the Midnight Express*
by Margaret K. Wetterer, illustrated by Karen Ritz.
Copyright © 1990 by Carolrhoda Books, Inc.

Printed in Singapore

ISBN   0-15-314356-8

3 4 5 6 7 8 9 10   068   03 02 01

Author's Note

Katherine Carroll Shelley, "Kate," was born in Ireland on September 25, 1865. Before she was a year old, her parents brought her to America. They bought a small farm near the town of Moingona, Iowa. Kate's father built a house overlooking Honey Creek, within sight of the Chicago and Northwestern Railroad line, and farmed the land. He also took a job with the railroad.

After Kate, there were four more children, James, Mayme, Margaret, and John. Life in the Shelleys' isolated cottage was hard but satisfying, full of good friends and good times.

Then, when Kate was 13, her father died. Less than a year later, 10-year-old James drowned in the Des Moines River. Mrs. Shelley never really recovered from these tragedies. Kate took over more and more responsibility for running the farm and caring for the younger children.

When a raging storm hit the Des Moines River valley and lives hung in the balance, Kate did not hesitate to face danger and go out alone into the night to do what she believed was her duty.

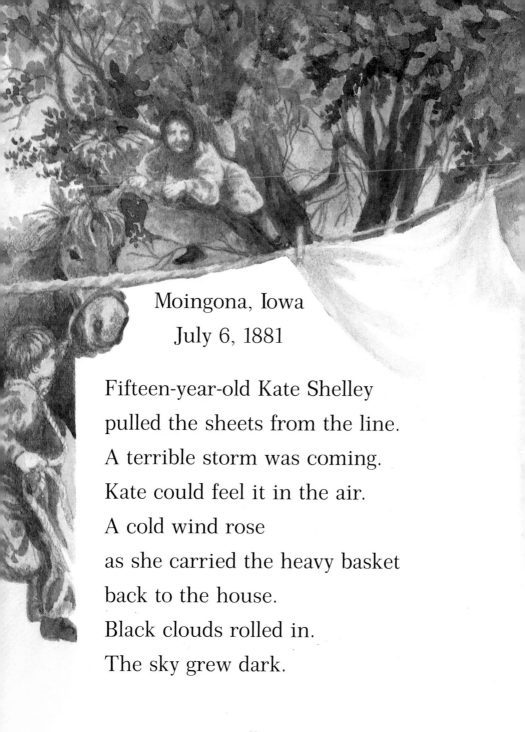

Moingona, Iowa
July 6, 1881

Fifteen-year-old Kate Shelley
pulled the sheets from the line.
A terrible storm was coming.
Kate could feel it in the air.
A cold wind rose
as she carried the heavy basket
back to the house.
Black clouds rolled in.
The sky grew dark.

Kate stood at the kitchen window
with her younger sisters and brother.
They saw lightning flash.
They heard thunder crack in the hills.
Then the rain came.

As the rain poured down,
they watched the water rising
in Honey Creek.
Soon it overflowed its banks
and flooded part of the yard.
"I'm going to let the animals
out of the barn," Kate said.
"If the water keeps rising,
they could drown."
"Be careful you don't slip in the water,"
her mother warned.

Kate ran down the hill.
She waded through muddy water
to the barn.
She led out the two horses
and shooed them off to higher ground.
She drove the cows up the hill.
Then she hurried back to the barn.
She picked up some piglets
and carried them to the house.
By this time, she was soaked to the skin.

Kate put on dry clothes
and went back to the window.
The rain had not let up.
The floodwater was coming closer
to the house.
When lightning flashed,
Kate could see
the shining railroad tracks.
They ran along
the other side of Honey Creek.
Kate peered through the rain,
trying to see the railroad bridge
over Honey Creek.
How was it holding up in this storm?

After supper,
the younger children went to bed.
Nine-year-old Mayme
wanted to stay awake
with her mother and Kate.
They sat at the kitchen table,
talking about the dangers of the storm.
They were worried about the men
out working on the railroad.

At midnight, an express train would pass
the Moingona station without stopping.
It would cross the long bridge
over the Des Moines River.
Then it would cross the bridge
over Honey Creek, near Kate's house.
Were the bridges safe?

Shortly after eleven o'clock,
Kate and her mother heard an engine
chugging slowly down the tracks.
Railroad men were checking
the tracks and bridges
before the express came through.
They were heading toward
the bridge over Honey Creek.

Suddenly, the engine's bell rang wildly.
Then Kate heard a terrible crack.
She knew at once
that the bridge had broken.

Kate heard the hot engine hiss
as it hit the cold water.
She jumped to her feet.
"Oh, Mother," she cried.
"They've gone down in Honey Creek.
I must go help."

The crash woke the children.
They watched silently
as Kate pulled on a jacket
and an old straw hat.
Then she lit
her father's railroad lantern.

"You can't go, Kate,"
her mother said.
"It's too dangerous."
"I have to go, Mother,"
Kate answered.
"Someone may still be alive
in Honey Creek.
And I have to stop the midnight express."
"Please, Kate," her mother cried.
"Don't go.
The floodwaters are almost at our door."

"If that were Father down there,
wouldn't we want someone to help him?"
asked Kate.
"You're right," her mother agreed.
"Go ahead then, but be careful!
We'll be praying for you."

Kate could not cross the flooded yard
to get to the broken bridge.
Instead, she started up a path
behind her house.
She would reach the tracks
where they ran through the hills.

Water poured down the hillside.
Kate climbed over fallen trees.
Her skirt caught in wet brambles.
Her shoes sank in mud.
But she held
her father's lantern before her
and kept going.
At last she reached the tracks.

Kate ran along the tracks
back to the broken bridge.
She looked out
over the dark waters of Honey Creek.
She could not see the engine
or any of the crew.
Had they all drowned?
Then Kate thought she heard a shout.
In the roar of the storm,
she was not sure.
She listened again.
Yes. Someone was calling.

Lightning flashed.
Kate saw someone holding on
to the branches of a treetop
just above the water.
Thunder boomed.
As it faded,
Kate heard voices calling again.

She could hear two men's voices now,
but she couldn't make out their words
above the howl of the storm.
"Hang on! Hang on!" Kate shouted.
"I'll get help."
Kate swung the lantern back and forth.
Now the men would know
she had heard them
and was going for help.

Kate began to run
toward the Moingona station.
There wasn't much time.
She had to get to the station
before midnight,
before the express.

Kate ran along the tracks.
Even before she reached
the Des Moines River bridge,
she could hear
the rush of the floodwater.
She held up the lantern
to light her way over the bridge.
But as she did,
a fierce wind blew out
the lantern's small flame.

Kate stared into the darkness.
To reach the Moingona station,
she had to cross this river.
The long wooden bridge
stretched before her.
Beside the tracks was a narrow walkway.
Some of its boards were missing.
There was no handrail to hold.
Kate was afraid to cross this bridge
even in daylight.
Could she do it now, in this storm,
in the dark?

Kate thought of the men
in Honey Creek.
She thought of all the people on the train
speeding toward the broken bridge.
She got down on her hands and knees
and began to crawl across.

Kate felt for gaps in the walkway
so she would not fall through.
Nails and splinters cut her hands
and knees and tore her skirt.
She gripped the steel rail of the tracks
to keep the wind
from sweeping her over the side.

Trees and logs in the flooded river
crashed against the bridge,
making it shake.
When she reached
the middle of the bridge,
great flashes of lightning
suddenly lit the night.
She looked up.
A huge tree was coming down the river
straight toward her.
Surely it would crash through the bridge.
Kate closed her eyes and prayed.

In the next moment,
the river pulled the tree
down under the water.
Kate felt the tree
scrape beneath the walkway.
Then it was gone.

Kate was shaking with fear,
but she could not stop to rest.
She knew it must be almost midnight.
She had to reach the station
before the midnight express.

At last, Kate's hand touched land.

She had crossed the river.

The Moingona station

was less than a half mile ahead.

She got to her feet and began to run.

Her heart pounded.

Her throat ached.

But through the rain,

she saw the lights of the station.

Kate threw open the station house door.
The men inside turned and stared.
Kate's clothes were torn and muddy.
Water dripped from her old straw hat.
She tried to speak,
but no words came.
At last she gasped,
"The engine went down in Honey Creek.
Stop the express."
Then she sagged to the floor.

"The girl must be crazy,"
someone said.

But the station agent knew Kate.
"She means a bridge is out,"
he shouted.
"We must stop the express."
He rushed to the telegraph
and tapped out a message to Ogden,
the station before Moingona.
STOP EXPRESS...BRIDGE OUT...
STOP EXPRESS

Another man grabbed a lantern.
Then he ran out to the platform.
He would flag down the express
if the telegraph message was too late.
The express,
with two hundred people aboard,
was still speeding
toward the broken bridge.

But Kate's warning had come on time.
Railroad men stopped the train at Ogden.
It was the last telegraph message
sent or received that night.
The storm knocked out telegraph service
for 40 miles along the line.
Someone helped Kate to a chair.
Someone gave her a glass of water.
"Two men are still alive
in Honey Creek," Kate said.
"I saw them holding on to trees
in the water."

"Let's try to save them
before they're washed away,"
a man said.
"Would you help us, Kate?"
another man asked.
"Would you show us where they are?"

Kate rode the engine
with the rescue party.
They crossed the Des Moines River
on the same bridge Kate had crawled over.
The engine stopped
at the broken bridge on Honey Creek.

Everyone shouted,
and the men in the water answered.
They were still hanging on.
But there was no way to reach them
from that side of the flooded creek.

Kate led the rescue party
into the hills behind her house.
She led them through the woods
to a bridge farther upstream.

There, they crossed Honey Creek
and at last rescued the two exhausted men.

Afterword

Kate went home and slept for a long time. When she awoke, her family, friends, and neighbors greeted her happily. They wanted to hear about her adventure. Reporters came. Newspapers across the country told the story of her bravery. Soon the whole nation knew about Kate Shelley. The railroad company gave Kate one hundred dollars and a lifetime pass on the railroad. Poems and songs were written in her honor. The State of Iowa awarded her a gold medal.

But of all the honors given to her, Kate liked the one from her railroad friends best. Whenever she rode the train home, they stopped it to let her off right in front of her own house.